The 30-Day Financial Freedom Challenge

Proudly Presented By:
- JWH Jr.

Legal Notice:- This book is for informational purposes only. While every attempt has been made to verify the information provided in this book, neither the author nor the distributor assume any responsibility for errors or omissions. Any slights of people or organizations are unintentional and the Development of this book is bona fide. This book has been distributed with the understanding that we are not engaged in rendering technical, legal, accounting or other professional advice. We do not give any kind of guarantee about the accuracy of information provided. In no event will the author and/or marketer be liable for any direct, indirect, incidental, consequential or other loss or damage arising out of the use of this document by any person, regardless of whether or not informed of the possibility of damages in advance.

Table of Contents

The 30-Day Financial Freedom Challenge..1
   Introduction: The Journey to Financial Freedom..3
   Chapter 1: Day One: Defining Your Financial Freedom..4
      What Does Financial Freedom Look Like?...4
      The Importance of Setting Specific Goals..5
      Creating Your Financial Freedom Vision Board..5
      The Role of Mindset in Achieving Financial Freedom...6
      Daily Reflection: Documenting Your Journey...6
      Final Thoughts..6
   Chapter 2: Day Two: Crafting Your Budget Blueprint...7
      Understanding the Purpose of a Budget..7
      Assessing Your Current Financial Situation...7
      Calculating Your Income..7
      Understanding and Categorizing Your Expenses...8
      Creating Expense Categories..8
      The 50/30/20 Budgeting Rule...9
      Creating Your Budget..9
      Track Your Spending...9
      Evaluating Your Budget: Flexibility is Important...10
      Final Thoughts..10
   Chapter 3: Day Three: Understanding Your Income and Expenses....................10
      The Importance of Knowing Your Income...10
         Identifying Your Income Sources...11
      Understanding Your Expenses in Detail...11
         Fixed vs. Variable Expenses...11
      Diving Deeper into Expense Tracking...12
         Review Past Statements...12
         Create a Spending Log..12
      Assessing Your Needs vs. Wants..12
      Building a Spending Plan...13
      Practice Mindful Spending..13
      Final Thoughts..13
   Chapter 4: Day Four: Tackling Debt: The Snowball and Avalanche Method.........14
      Understanding Your Debt..14
      The Snowball Method: Small Steps to Big Wins...15
         Steps for the Snowball Method..15
      The Avalanche Method: Saving on Interest..15
         Steps for the Avalanche Method..16
      Choosing Your Debt Repayment Strategy..16
      Discovering Strategies to Accelerate Debt Payoff..16
      Building an Emergency Fund for Added Security..17
      The Power of Accountability..17
      Final Thoughts..17

- Chapter 5: Day Five: Building an Emergency Fund 17
  - Why You Need an Emergency Fund 18
  - How Much to Save 18
  - Setting Up a Separate Savings Account 18
  - How to Build Your Emergency Fund 19
  - Finding Ways to Save More 19
  - Tapping Into Your Fund: When and How 20
  - Final Thoughts 20
- Chapter 6: Day Six: Smart Saving Strategies 20
  - The Importance of Saving Wisely 21
  - Setting Clear Savings Goals 21
  - Choosing the Right Savings Account 21
  - Automating Your Savings 22
  - Finding Extra Funds to Save 22
  - The 50/30/20 Rule Revisited 23
  - Invest in Your Future: The Power of Compound Interest 23
  - Review and Adjust Regularly 23
  - Final Thoughts 23
- Chapter 7: Day Seven: Introduction to Investing 24
  - Why Invest? 24
  - Understanding Risk and Return 24
  - Different Investment Avenues 25
  - Getting Started with Investing 26
  - The Power of Dollar-Cost Averaging 26
  - Regularly Review Your Investments 26
  - Final Thoughts 27
- Chapter 8: Day Eight: Creating Passive Income Streams 27
  - What is Passive Income? 27
  - Why Create Passive Income Streams? 27
  - Types of Passive Income Streams 28
  - How to Get Started with Passive Income 29
  - Keeping it Sustainable 29
  - Planned Growth 29
  - Final Thoughts 30

Introduction: The Journey to Financial Freedom

Welcome to "The 30-Day Financial Freedom Challenge!" If you picked up this book, you might be feeling overwhelmed by your finances or, perhaps, you're simply looking to enhance your financial literacy and build a stronger foundation for your future. Whatever your reasons are, you're in the right place! Over the next month, we'll explore the essential steps you can take to transform your relationship with money.

Many of us have been taught to think of money as something we earn to spend, but this mindset often leads to stress, anxiety, and financial instability. The challenge we face is figuring out how to use money as a tool to create a life of abundance, security, and most importantly, freedom. Financial freedom means different things to different people. For some, it's living debt-free; for others, it's the ability to retire early or travel whenever they want.

Throughout this book, we'll dive into practical, hands-on strategies that empower you to take control of your financial destiny. Each chapter is designed to be straightforward and actionable, allowing you to tackle one crucial aspect of your finances each day. Throughout the journey, you'll be guided through budgeting, saving, investing, and so much more—all intended to align you with your personal definition of financial freedom.

You might wonder why a 30-day challenge, and that's a great question! The truth is, breaking down your financial journey into manageable steps is a powerful way to make real, lasting changes. It's easy to feel overwhelmed when looking at your finances as a whole, but focusing on one aspect each day will make the process feel more attainable—and even enjoyable!

Keep in mind that achieving financial freedom requires commitment. You will need to invest time, effort, and emotional energy into undertaking this challenge. However, I promise you, the rewards you'll reap will far outweigh your initial investment. Each day will build on the previous one, leading you to a comprehensive understanding of personal finance.

Financial freedom is not just about numbers; it's a mindset shift. Instead of behaving reactively with your money, you'll learn to take the driver's seat, empowering yourself to make choices that align with your long-term goals and values.

So, grab a notebook, a cup of your favorite beverage, and get ready to take the first step toward mastering your money in a way that feels right for you. The practices you'll learn are tools for your financial toolkit, to be used for a lifetime ahead.

Remember, you're not alone on this journey. Many others are navigating similar paths and challenges. As you engage with this challenge and implement the strategies we discuss, you'll not only cultivate financial skills but also build confidence and a supportive community of like-minded individuals. Let's get started on your path to financial freedom—your future self will thank you!

Chapter 1: Day One: Defining Your Financial Freedom

On the journey to financial freedom, the very first step (and arguably one of the most important) is defining what financial freedom means to you personally. If I were to ask you to imagine a life where your financial situation no longer caused you stress, what would it look like? Would it entail living debt-free? Having six months of expenses saved in the bank? Perhaps it means traveling the world, retiring early, or even living in your dream home. It's essential to pinpoint your own definition because this will serve as your guiding star throughout the next 30 days.

What Does Financial Freedom Look Like?

Let's dive deeper into your vision. Picture yourself three to five years down the line: What do you see? Perhaps you picture a life where you work solely for enjoyment, not out of necessity. You might envision a cozy home filled with loved ones, vacations to places you've always dreamed of, or the ability to donate to causes that matter to you without worry. Each individual has a unique vision, and take this moment to jot down yours.

The Importance of Setting Specific Goals

Once you have a broad vision, it's time to translate that into specific, actionable goals. The SMART criteria is an excellent framework to guide you in this process. SMART stands for Specific, Measurable, Achievable, Relevant, and Time-bound.

Specific: Instead of saying you want to "save more money," state how much you wish to save within a specific timeframe—"I will save $5,000 for a family vacation in the next 12 months."

Measurable: Establish a way to measure your progress. This could involve tracking your savings in a dedicated app or spreadsheet.

Achievable: Ensure your goal is realistic considering your current financial situation. If you're starting from zero savings, aiming for $100,000 in a year may be unrealistic.

Relevant: Your goals should align with your vision of financial freedom. Ask yourself if each goal brings you closer to that dream life.

Time-bound: Assign a deadline to your goal. This creates a sense of urgency, motivating you to work steadily towards it.

Creating Your Financial Freedom Vision Board

Visual aids can be powerful, as they give concrete representation to your aspirations. A vision board allows you to compile images, quotes, and reminders that resonate with your goals for financial freedom. Spend a creative evening cutting out pictures from magazines or printing images from the internet that represent elements of your dream life—whether it's a new car, a home in the countryside, or tropical beach vacations.

By placing your vision board somewhere you see daily, you keep yourself reminded and motivated about your financial journey.

The Role of Mindset in Achieving Financial Freedom

It's crucial to cultivate a positive mindset about money. Limiting beliefs often hold people back from their financial aspirations. Maybe you've told yourself that money doesn't grow on trees or that wealthy people are greedy. Whatever these beliefs may be, challenge them.

Instead, replace those thoughts with affirmations focused on abundance and worthiness: "I attract opportunities," or "I am capable of managing my finances wisely." Acknowledge your strengths and what you bring to the table; everyone has the capability to improve their financial situation.

Daily Reflection: Documenting Your Journey

Every day for the next 30 days, take time to reflect on your progress. Consider keeping a financial journal where you write down your goals, feelings, and any challenges you face. This is an invaluable tool that will help keep you grounded and motivated. Over time, you will appreciate the growth and learning that occurs.

Final Thoughts

As we embark on this 30-day challenge together, remember that every step counts, no matter how small. With clear goals and a fresh mindset, you're setting yourself up for monumental success. Financial freedom is not merely about the dollars and cents in your bank account; it's about the freedom to live on your terms. Embrace the journey, stay committed to your vision, and know that the first day is only the beginning. Your future self will be grateful for the efforts you put in today!

Chapter 2: Day Two: Crafting Your Budget Blueprint

Welcome to Day Two! Now that you're clear on what financial freedom looks like for you and have set actionable goals, let's get practical by crafting your budget blueprint. A budget is one of the most powerful tools at your disposal; it serves as both a roadmap and a reality check, keeping you on track with your financial goals.

Understanding the Purpose of a Budget

At its core, a budget is a plan for how you will spend and save your money over a given period, usually on a monthly basis. The purpose of budgeting is to ensure that you have enough money for the things that matter most, whether that's your top priorities in life, paying off debt, funding your savings, or enjoying entertainment and leisure activities.

A well-crafted budget empowers you to live within your means while also giving you the ability to allocate funds towards your financial goals. Budgeting is not about deprivation; it's about intentional spending and making informed choices.

Assessing Your Current Financial Situation

Before diving into budget creation, it's crucial to take stock of your current financial situation. Gather the following documents:

- Recent bank statements
- Credit card statements
- Monthly bills
- Pay stubs or income documentation

Now, you can calculate your total income and expenses. This will inform how much you can responsibly allocate towards savings and investment, address any debts, and fund your lifestyle.

Calculating Your Income

Your income isn't limited to just your paycheck. Include any additional sources of income such as:

- Side jobs or freelance work
- Bonuses, overtime, or commissions
- Passive income streams (like rental income or dividends)
- Government benefits or assistance

Once you've listed all sources, total them for your monthly income.

Understanding and Categorizing Your Expenses

Next, it's time to identify your expenses. These can be divided into fixed and variable expenses:

1. **Fixed Expenses**: These expenses remain relatively constant each month, such as rent, mortgage payments, auto loans, insurance premiums, and subscriptions.
2. **Variable Expenses**: These can fluctuate and include groceries, dining out, entertainment, and transportation costs.

Creating Expense Categories

Categorizing your expenses helps facilitate your budgeting process and allows for clearer tracking of spending habits. Consider using categories such as:

- Housing
- Utilities
- Food
- Health and wellness
- Transportation

> Debt payments
> Savings/Investments
> Entertainment

Having these categories will help you visualize where your money is going and identify areas for potential savings.

The 50/30/20 Budgeting Rule

One effective budgeting method to consider is the 50/30/20 rule. This rule suggests allocating:

> **50% of your income** towards needs (essentials like housing, food, health).
> **30% towards wants** (non-essential expenses like dining out, entertainment, and hobbies).
> **20% towards savings and debt repayment** (this can be savings for an emergency fund, retirement, or paying off credit cards).

This approach is straightforward and flexible while still encouraging opportunities for both enjoyment and financial building.

Creating Your Budget

Now that you have a clear picture of your income and your categorized expenses, it's time to create your budget. You can use various methods here:

1. **Pen and Paper**: Traditional, but it allows for a tactile experience.
2. **Spreadsheets**: Excel or Google Sheets can be valuable for tracking over time and calculating totals easily.
3. **Budgeting Apps**: Applications like Mint, YNAB (You Need A Budget), or EveryDollar can streamline budgeting and offer alerts and categories.

Whichever method you choose, ensure it resonates with your needs and feels comfortable for you.

Track Your Spending

Once your budget is in place, tracking your actual spending is vital. Each time you spend money, record it to visualize how well you're staying within your budget. This can be done daily or weekly, but consistency is key.

Evaluating Your Budget: Flexibility is Important

Your first draft won't be perfect, and that's okay! Life is unpredictable, and expenses may vary. At the end of each month, evaluate your budget. Ask yourself:

> Did I stick to my budget?
> Where did I overspend or underspend?
> What categories require more adjustment next month?

Adjust as needed until you find a budget that works well for you.

Final Thoughts

Congratulations! You've created your budget blueprint, which is a massive step towards achieving financial freedom. A solid budget will help you see your finances with clarity, allow for better decision-making, and encourage healthy spending habits. Embrace this new approach to managing your money with a positive mindset, and remember: this is a journey, not a sprint. With your budget laid out, you'll be prepared for tomorrow's topic: understanding your income and expenses in more detail.

Chapter 3: Day Three: Understanding Your Income and Expenses

Welcome to Day Three of your financial freedom journey! Now that you've crafted a budget blueprint, let's take a closer look at the heart of your financial life: your income and expenses. Understanding these key components is crucial for a comprehensive grasp of your financial health.

The Importance of Knowing Your Income

Your income forms the foundation from which you will build your financial portrait. This is the money you bring in every month, and knowing its sources, amounts, and predictability is vital.

Identifying Your Income Sources

Make a comprehensive list of all income sources. As mentioned in Day Two, this includes:

Primary Job: Salary or hourly wage. Make sure to note your take-home pay (net income) after tax deductions.
Side Hustles: Supplemental income from freelancing, part-time jobs, or gigs.
Investment Income: Any dividends, interest, or profits from investments in stocks or real estate.
Passive Income: Money generated with little effort. Think royalties from creative work, income from rental properties, or earnings from affiliate marketing.

By listing these income sources, you'll gain a clearer perspective on your overall financial picture.

Understanding Your Expenses in Detail

Now, let's dive deeper into your expenses. Your expenses can impact how much of your income remains available for saving and investing, so it's essential to track them meticulously.

Fixed vs. Variable Expenses

As a quick recap, expenses can be categorized into two main types:

Fixed Expenses: These are necessary and usually inflexible costs you incur month after month. They often include your rent or mortgage, insurance, loan payments, and subscriptions.

Variable Expenses: These expenses can fluctuate from month to month and often include groceries, gas, entertainment, and dining out.

Diving Deeper into Expense Tracking

To effectively manage your budget, you'll want to scrutinize your spending habits, particularly in variable expense areas. Here's how to get started:

Review Past Statements

Take the time to look back over your past bank and credit card statements for the last three to six months. This will help you identify patterns in your spending.

High Spending Categories: Look for categories where you tend to overspend compared to your budget. Are you spending more on dining out than you anticipated?

Trends and Patterns: Are there specific times of the month when you tend to spend more?

Create a Spending Log

Maintain a spending log for one month to capture every expense, no matter how small. This can help you become more conscious of your spending and identify trends or triggers for overspending.

Logging Techniques: You can use a simple notebook, a budgeting app, or even an Excel spreadsheet. Ensure you categorize your expenditures to match your budget.

Assessing Your Needs vs. Wants

A critical part of managing income and expenses is distinguishing between needs and wants.

Needs: Necessities required for your day-to-day living; this includes food, housing, insurance, and healthcare.

Wants: Discretionary expenses that enhance your life but are not necessary for survival; examples include dining out, entertainment options like movies, vacations, or subscription services.

Understanding this distinction helps in rationalizing your spending decisions. When you evaluate an expense, ask yourself whether it is a genuine need or just a want.

Building a Spending Plan

Once you have a clearer understanding of your income and expenses, it's essential to build a spending plan that works for you. Here are some tips:

Prioritize Your Needs: Allocate your income first to cover your fixed needs before addressing your variable expenses and wants.

Set Limits on Variable Expenses: Based on your past spending patterns, set realistic limits for variable expenses.

Account for Irregular Expenses: Don't forget to factor in the irregular expenses that might not occur monthly, such as insurance premiums, car maintenance, or annual memberships. Set aside small amounts each month in a sinking fund to cover these expenses when they arise.

Practice Mindful Spending

Mindful spending means being aware of your purchasing decisions and their impact on your overall financial goals. Before making a purchase, ask yourself the following questions:

Is this what I truly need right now?
Does this align with my financial goals?
How will this affect my budget?

Final Thoughts

Today's focus was about understanding the raw materials of your financial life: your income and expenses. By pinpointing and analyzing these components, you establish a clear baseline from which you can move forward. As we progress into the next chapter, we'll tackle the pressing issue of debt, a common roadblock to financial freedom. Remember, knowledge is power. You're gaining insights that will profoundly impact your financial future!

Chapter 4: Day Four: Tackling Debt: The Snowball and Avalanche Method

Welcome to Day Four of your financial freedom challenge! Congratulations on making it this far. Today, we tackle one of the most significant barriers many people face on the road to financial independence: debt. Whether it's credit card balances, student loans, or other types of loans, dealing with debt can be overwhelming. But fear not! With the right strategies, you can conquer it.

Understanding Your Debt

Before we jump into strategies, it's essential to understand what types of debt you are dealing with. Typically, debt can be classified into two main categories:

1. **Good Debt**: This is debt that can help you create opportunities or provide benefits in the long run. Think mortgages (in homes that appreciate), student loans for education, or business loans that can lead to increased income.

2. **Bad Debt**: This debt does not grow your net worth or lead to opportunities; instead, it often costs you more in interest over time. Examples include credit card debt for frivolous purchases or high-interest personal loans.

Start by making a list of all your debts. Record the following information for each item:

Creditor: Who do you owe?
Total Amount Owed: The total balance for that debt.
Minimum Monthly Payment: The lowest amount you need to pay each month.
Interest Rate: This will help prioritize which debts to focus on first.

The Snowball Method: Small Steps to Big Wins

The snowball method is a popular debt repayment strategy centered around quick wins. The idea is to focus on paying off your smallest debts first while making the minimum payments on larger debts.

Steps for the Snowball Method

1. **List Your Debts**: Arrange your debts from the smallest balance to the largest.
2. **Make Minimum Payments**: Ensure you're making at least the minimum payments on all debts except the smallest.
3. **Focus Extra Payments on the Smallest Debt**: Channel any extra money you can toward the smallest debt. This could mean reallocating funds from your budget, cutting back on non-essential expenses, or picking up side hustles to generate additional income.
4. **Celebrate Milestones**: Once you pay off your smallest debt, celebrate the victory! Use that momentum to tackle the next smallest debt in your list, using the payments from the first to help pay down the second.

The snowball method relies on behavioral psychology. The quick wins provide a motivational boost, encouraging you to keep going as you see debts vanish.

The Avalanche Method: Saving on Interest

For those who want to focus on saving the most money possible (especially on interest), the avalanche method could be the better choice. This method encourages you to pay off debts with the highest interest rates first, saving you money in the long run.

Steps for the Avalanche Method

1. **List Your Debts**: Arrange your debts from the highest interest rate to the lowest.
2. **Make Minimum Payments**: As with the snowball method, ensure you're making the minimum payments on all debts except for the one with the highest interest rate.
3. **Focus Extra Payments on the Highest Debt**: Direct any extra money toward the highest-interest debt until it's gone. Then move to the next highest.

Although the avalanche method may lack the quick wins of the snowball method, the savings from lower interest payments can have a pronounced long-term effect.

Choosing Your Debt Repayment Strategy

Both methods are effective, but choosing the right approach depends on your personality and financial situation. If you find motivation in quick wins, you may lean toward the snowball method. If you're more analytical and focused on numbers, you might prefer the avalanche method.

Discovering Strategies to Accelerate Debt Payoff

Here are some strategies you can use to speed up your debt repayment process:

Cut Unnecessary Expenses: Review your budget to see where you can cut back on non-essential spending. Channel these savings directly toward your debt payments.

Increase Your Income: Consider taking on a part-time job, freelance gigs, or selling unused items around your house to raise funds.

Reassess Your Financial Goals: Ensure your financial goals are in line with your debt-reduction efforts. This may involve temporarily halting non-essential saving goals until your debt is under control.

Consider Negotiating Your Interest Rates: Contact creditors to negotiate better interest rates. If you have a solid payment history, they may be willing to accommodate you.

Building an Emergency Fund for Added Security

As you focus on paying off debts, it can be beneficial to build a small emergency fund (if you haven't already) to avoid further debt accumulation due to unforeseen expenses.

Aim for a fund of at least $500-$1,000 initially, so you have a buffer for emergencies without needing to rely on credit cards.

The Power of Accountability

Consider finding an accountability partner to support you in your debt payoff journey. This could be a friend, family member, or even a group. Sharing goals and progress can bolster motivation and encourage consistency.

Final Thoughts

Congratulations! Today, you've learned how to tackle one of the most significant financial hurdles—debt. By deciding on a repayment strategy and understanding the dynamics of debt, you're one step closer to achieving financial freedom. Tomorrow, we'll focus on one of the cornerstones of financial health: building an emergency fund. Keep pushing forward; you're doing great!

Chapter 5: Day Five: Building an Emergency Fund

Welcome to Day Five of your financial freedom challenge! Today, we'll discuss one of the most crucial aspects of personal finance: building an emergency fund. Having a safety net can be a game-changer when it comes to achieving financial security and peace of mind.

Why You Need an Emergency Fund

Life is full of surprises—some delightful and others, well, not so much. An emergency fund is designed to cushion the financial blow of unexpected events such as:

- Job loss
- Medical emergencies
- Major car repairs
- Unexpected home repairs

By having money set aside specifically for emergencies, you can navigate these situations with less stress and without derailing your financial plan.

How Much to Save

The general rule of thumb is to aim for three to six months' worth of living expenses. However, this amount can vary based on individual circumstances:

Job Security: If your job is stable and secure, three months of expenses might suffice.
Instability: If you work in an industry known for volatility or if your job is contract-based, consider aiming for closer to six months or more.

Family Considerations: If you're the sole breadwinner for your household, you may want a more substantial fund to ensure your family's needs are covered.

Setting Up a Separate Savings Account

Creating a dedicated savings account for your emergency fund can help keep your money separate from your day-to-day finances. Here are some tips for setting it up:

Choose a High-Yield Savings Account: Look for accounts that offer higher interest rates to make the most of your savings while still allowing easy access.

Keep it Separate: Do not mix emergency funds with your regular savings or checking accounts. This will help minimize the temptation to dip into your emergency fund for non-emergencies.

Consider Accessibility, but Avoid Instant Access: It's crucial to keep the funds accessible but not so easy to withdraw that you're tempted to use them for everyday purchases.

How to Build Your Emergency Fund

1. **Set a Goal**: Define how much you want in your emergency fund. Then, break that down into smaller monthly or weekly goals.
2. **Automate Savings**: Set up automatic transfers from your checking account to your emergency fund account, ensuring you contribute regularly.
3. **Start Small**: If saving a significant amount feels overwhelming, begin with a smaller goal, such as $500, and gradually increase it over time.
4. **Find Extra Money**: Look for opportunities to fund your emergency savings. Whether it's redirecting part of your paycheck, cutting back on discretionary spending, or using tax refunds, find ways to boost your savings.

Finding Ways to Save More

Here are some actionable tips for identifying extra funds to contribute to your emergency savings:

Review Your Budget: Look for areas where you can cut back—this could be dining out less frequently, canceling subscriptions you don't use, or finding cheaper alternatives to your usual purchases.
Cash Windfalls: When you receive a bonus at work, gifted money, or any unplanned windfall, consider allocating a portion to your emergency fund.
Plan a Saving Challenge: Try a 30-day saving challenge where you save a small amount daily, gradually increasing the amount each week. There are many variations of this challenge, but the idea is to make saving fun and motivating!

Tapping Into Your Fund: When and How

Knowing when to tap into your emergency fund is essential. Only use it for genuine emergencies—here's what qualifies as an emergency:

Medical emergencies—unforeseen healthcare costs.
Replace essential car repairs that impact your safety or ability to work.
Out-of-pocket costs when experiencing a job loss or unexpected unemployment.

Once you take funds from your emergency fund, prioritize replenishing it. Accountability to yourself is vital here.

Final Thoughts

Today, you've taken a significant step toward financial security by building your emergency fund plan. In a world full of uncertainties, having this safety net will give you peace of mind and freedom from worrying about unforeseen expenses. Tomorrow, we'll begin exploring smart saving strategies to put your money to work for you and grow your wealth. Keep moving forward; you're doing an amazing job!

Chapter 6: Day Six: Smart Saving Strategies

Welcome to Day Six of your financial freedom journey! With your emergency fund set up (or on the way!), it's time to dive into a crucial aspect of financial health: smart saving strategies. Learning how to save effectively can help you achieve your financial goals faster and make your money work for you.

The Importance of Saving Wisely

Saving money is more than just stashing away a portion of your income; it's about having a strategy that aligns with your goals. Saving wisely means ensuring your savings grow over time and are accessible when needed.

Setting Clear Savings Goals

Before you start saving, it's essential to establish clear goals. Specific, measurable goals help you create a targeted saving strategy. Here's how to think about your savings goals:

1. **Short-Term Goals**: These are typically goals you wish to achieve within a year. Examples include saving for a vacation, a new car, or holiday expenses.
2. **Medium-Term Goals**: These usually span one to five years. Perhaps you're saving for a down payment on a house or furthering your education.
3. **Long-Term Goals**: These are anything taking five years or more. This could encompass retirement savings, children's education funds, or large investments.

Choosing the Right Savings Account

Once you've set your goals, the next step is to choose the right savings account or investment vehicle. Here are different options based on your savings timeline:

1. **High-Yield Savings Accounts**: An excellent option for short to medium-term savings goals, high-yield saving accounts provide better interest compared to standard savings accounts.
2. **Certificates of Deposit (CDs)**: If you can commit to leaving your money untouched for a predetermined amount of time, consider CDs. They often offer higher interest rates compared to regular savings accounts.
3. **Money Market Accounts**: These accounts tend to offer higher interest rates than standard savings accounts and come with check-writing privileges, making them a good choice for your emergency fund or short-term savings.
4. **Investment Accounts**: For long-term savings goals, investing in stocks, bonds, or mutual funds might be appropriate. While these options come with risks, they typically yield higher returns over time than traditional savings accounts.

Automating Your Savings

One of the easiest ways to save is by automating the process. Setting up automatic transfers from your checking account to your savings account (or investment accounts) can help you save without even thinking about it.

Budgeting: Include your savings in your monthly budget as a non-negotiable expense. Treating savings like any other fixed expense will help ensure you prioritize it.

Finding Extra Funds to Save

If you're struggling to find room in your budget to save, here are some tips to uncover extra funds:

Use Windfalls Wisely: Tax refunds, bonuses, or unexpected income should be viewed as opportunities to boost your savings, rather than spent on immediate desires.

Cut Back on Non-Essentials: Carefully review your expenses. Identify subscriptions you don't use or dining out habits that can be limited. Even small savings can accumulate over time!

The 50/30/20 Rule Revisited

As discussed in Chapter 2, revisit the 50/30/20 budgeting rule, focusing on channeling your 20% towards savings and investments. Rearranging your budget accordingly can pave the way for disciplined savings.

Invest in Your Future: The Power of Compound Interest

Understanding compound interest is essential when it comes to savings and investments. The sooner you start saving, the more time your money has to grow. Here's how it works:

What is Compound Interest?: The interest on your savings earns interest over time. This means that as your savings grow, the amount of money your investment earns also increases—essentially creating a snowball effect.

Start Early: For example, if you save $100 a month and earn 5% interest over ten years, you'll have more than $12,500, thanks to the power of compounding.

Review and Adjust Regularly

Savings goals can change based on your life's circumstances. Regularly review your savings goals to ensure you're on track and that your strategies are aligned with your current situation. Adapt as necessary to stay focused on your financial freedom journey.

Final Thoughts

Congratulations on learning smart saving strategies today! Building wealth requires not only saving but saving wisely, ensuring you're actively working towards your goals. In our next chapter, we'll introduce a vital topic: investing. Get ready to explore the world of investment options that can help you grow your money over time. You're making fantastic progress; keep up the great work!

Chapter 7: Day Seven: Introduction to Investing

Welcome to Day Seven of your financial freedom challenge! If you've made it this far, you're developing an impressive foundation for financial literacy. Today, we'll take an exciting step forward by introducing you to the world of investing. Investing is one of the crucial components of building wealth, and understanding it can propel you toward your financial goals.

Why Invest?

You may wonder: Why should I focus on investing when I'm already budgeting and saving? Investing allows your money to grow over time, outpacing inflation and potentially increasing your purchasing power. Here are some key reasons why investing is important:

1. **Wealth Growth**: Investing can significantly increase your wealth over time. The potential for compounded returns means that the earlier you start, the more money you can accumulate.
2. **Beat Inflation**: Inflation can erode the purchasing power of your savings. By investing, you can generate returns that outpace inflation, ensuring your money retains its value over time.

3. **Achieve Financial Goals**: Investing plays a critical role in funding long-term financial goals, such as retirement, a child's education, or financial independence.

Understanding Risk and Return

Whenever you invest your money, it comes with an inherent risk: the potential for loss or the non-fulfillment of your expected return. In general, higher potential returns come with higher risks. As an investor, it's essential to understand your risk tolerance, which is influenced by your financial situation, investment goals, and overall comfort level with uncertainty.

Low-Risk Investments: These generally offer lower returns, such as savings accounts, CDs, and government bonds.

Moderate-Risk Investments: Stocks and mutual funds that carry some risks but can provide better growth potential.

High-Risk Investments: Options and cryptocurrencies, which can offer substantial returns but carry a greater potential for loss.

Different Investment Avenues

Now, let's explore some popular investment options:

1. **Stocks**: When you buy stocks, you are purchasing partial ownership of a company. Stocks offer the potential for high returns, but they also come with high volatility.
2. **Bonds**: Bonds are debt securities that represent a loan from you to a borrower (usually government or corporate). They typically offer fixed interest rates and are considered safer than stocks.
3. **Mutual Funds**: These are pooled investment vehicles managed by professionals that invest in various stocks, bonds, or other securities. They provide easy diversification and professional management for your investments.

4. **Exchange-Traded Funds (ETFs)**: Similar to mutual funds, but traded on exchanges like stocks. They generally have lower fees and are ideal for diversifying your portfolio.
5. **Real Estate**: Investing in real estate can include purchasing rental properties, REITs (real estate investment trusts), or flipping houses for profit. This can offer both cash flow and potential appreciation.
6. **Retirement Accounts**: Accounts like 401(k)s and IRAs offer tax advantages for retirement savings. These are excellent vehicles for long-term investing.

Getting Started with Investing

If you're ready to dip your toes into the world of investing, here's how to get started:

1. **Educate Yourself**: Read books, take online courses, or listen to finance podcasts. Increased knowledge will boost your confidence.
2. **Start Small**: You don't need thousands of dollars to start investing. Many platforms let you begin with minimal investments or allow micro-investing.
3. **Choose an Investment Account**: You'll need to open an investment account, such as a brokerage account or a retirement account. Research and compare fees and features to select the right option for you.
4. **Determine Your Investment Strategy**: Decide how you want to invest—whether that's choosing individual stocks, a mix of funds, or a passive approach like robo-advisors that automate portfolio management.
5. **Diversify Your Portfolio**: Don't put all your eggs in one basket. Diversifying across different asset classes and sectors can reduce risk and improve the potential for stable returns.

The Power of Dollar-Cost Averaging

As you embark on your investment journey, consider employing dollar-cost averaging. This strategy entails investing a fixed amount of money regularly, regardless of market conditions. This approach can reduce the impact of market volatility, as you purchase more shares when prices are low and fewer shares when prices are high.

Regularly Review Your Investments

Once you've begun investing, it's crucial to review and reassess your portfolio regularly to ensure it aligns with your current goals and risk tolerance. Market fluctuations may require rebalancing to maintain your desired asset allocation.

Final Thoughts

Congratulations! You've taken a significant step by learning about investing. Understanding this portion of finance not only empowers you but also opens doors to building long-term wealth and reaching your financial goals. Tomorrow, we'll explore creating passive income streams, allowing you to make money work for you even more effectively. Keep the momentum going—you're doing fantastic!

Chapter 8: Day Eight: Creating Passive Income Streams

Welcome to Day Eight of your journey towards financial freedom! By now, you've established a solid foundation in budgeting, saving, debt management, and investing. Today, we're going to discuss an essential aspect of building wealth: creating passive income streams. Learning to earn money while you sleep is a game-changer when it comes to achieving financial independence.

What is Passive Income?

Passive income is money earned with little to no effort on a recurring basis. Unlike active income, derived from working (like your salary), passive income requires an upfront investment—whether in time, money, or effort. The goal is to set it up so that it generates income over time with minimal maintenance.

Why Create Passive Income Streams?

1. **Financial Freedom**: Passive income can enable you to cover monthly expenses without having to actively work.
2. **Multiple Income Sources**: Diversifying your income sources can shield you from the risk of losing a job or income.
3. **Time for Other Pursuits**: With passive income, you can pursue other ventures, hobbies, or even spend more time with loved ones.

Types of Passive Income Streams

There are various avenues by which you can create passive income. Here's a rundown of some popular options:

1. **Real Estate Investments**: Rental income from property can generate a steady cash flow. You could also consider Real Estate Investment Trusts (REITs), which offer exposure to real estate without requiring you to manage properties.
2. **Dividend Stocks**: Investing in dividend-paying stocks can provide you with regular income distributions, typically on a quarterly basis. Reinvest dividends for compounding growth or use them as income.
3. **Peer-to-Peer Lending**: This involves lending money to individuals or businesses through online platforms that connect investors with borrowers. You earn interest on the loans over time.
4. **Create an Online Course**: If you possess a skill or expertise in a specific area, consider creating an online course. After the initial

effort of creating the course, you can earn income as students enroll.

5. **Write a Book or E-book**: Your thoughts and expertise can be transformed into a book or e-book. Once published, you earn royalties for each copy sold.
6. **Affiliate Marketing**: Starting a blog or website can provide opportunities for affiliate marketing. You earn commissions by promoting other companies' products or services and receiving a cut from sales generated through your links.
7. **Create a Mobile App**: If you have technical skills, consider developing a mobile app that provides value to users. You can earn money through purchases, ads, or premium features.
8. **Invest in a Business**: Consider investing in a business that offers the potential for passive income, like franchises or partnerships where you're not involved in day-to-day operations.

How to Get Started with Passive Income

1. **Identify Your Interests and Skills**: Your interests and skills can help you decide which passive income stream aligns best with you. Choosing something you're passionate about can keep you motivated in the long run.
2. **Research Options**: Explore different passive income ideas, and analyze their potential risks and rewards. Make sure to familiarize yourself with what's involved before diving in.
3. **Invest Time or Money**: Depending on the passive income stream you choose, allocate either the necessary time or money. For example, creating a course requires substantial upfront work, whereas investing in dividend stocks may require capital.
4. **Automate Your Income**: Wherever possible, automate your processes. Consider setting up systems that streamline payment processing or delivery so that you can minimize your involvement.

5. **Network and Learn**: Connect with others who are successfully creating passive income. They can share insights and support your journey.

Keeping it Sustainable

While passive income holds many benefits, it's essential to approach it with the understanding that sustainable income streams often take time to establish. Patience will be your ally as you embark on this journey.

Planned Growth

As your financial journey progresses:

Continue Improving: Constantly look for ways to enhance your knowledge and skills related to passive income.
Evaluate Performance: Regularly review your passive income streams to ensure they're aligned with your financial goals.

Final Thoughts

Congratulations! Today, you learned about the exciting world of passive income—an excellent way to enhance your financial future. Passive income offers the potential for freedom and flexibility, allowing you to generate income independent of your time and labor. In the coming days, keep applying your newfound knowledge as we move toward greater financial empowerment. Remember, each step you take brings you closer to your vision of financial freedom. Keep up the fantastic work!

www.ingramcontent.com/pod-product-compliance
Lightning Source LLC
Chambersburg PA
CBHW051536240526
45471CB00020B/3104